Let the Rainbow Shine

Getting to Know the LGBT Community

By Sydney Brown

Let the Rainbow Shine

GETTING TO KNOW THE LGBT COMMUNITY

by Sydney Brown

Published by TLM Publishing House

5905 Atlanta Highway, Alpharetta GA.
https://www.ttpublishinghouse.com
Copyright © 2023 TLM Publishing House

Dedication

To those who lived their lives in secret,
In the shadows of a world where freedom
was denied, this book is dedicated to you.

In generations past, when being LGBT
was met with fear, you navigated a
treacherous path, struggling against the
weight of societal expectations,
concealing your true selves, and yearning
to be free.

Today, we stand on the shoulders of your
resilience, witnessing the progress that
has been made. Yet, we must
acknowledge that our journey is far from
complete.

Though the world has changed and
acceptance has grown, there are still
corners where prejudice lingers, where

discrimination persists, and where love is met with intolerance.

We honor your courage, strength, and sacrifice for living your truth in a world that did not always embrace you.

Your stories, whispered through time, have shaped our understanding, kindling a fire within us to strive for a better tomorrow.

In your memory, we pledge to carry the torch of progress, to fight for a world where no one must hide, where every individual can love openly and authentically without fear of judgment or retribution.

We recognize the beauty of diversity, the power in unity, and the strength in lifting our voices together.

To those who lived in the shadows, your legacy lives on, guiding us as we continue to challenge prejudice, break down barriers, and create a brighter future.

This dedication is a tribute to you. To your resilience, your strength, and to the countless others who walked this path before us.

May we honor your memory by speaking our truths, amplifying our voices, and forging a world where every individual is celebrated, and every love is cherished.

Together, we will continue the journey until every person can live freely and authentically.

With gratitude and determination, we dedicate this book to you.

Let the Rainbow Shine: Getting to Know the LGBT Community

Acknowledgment

I'd like to thank the many new and existing friends who helped me with research and to make sure I wouldn't *open mouth- insert foot.*

The reality is that the LGBT community is so vast that it's tough (and arguably wrong) to try to put so many different people into any group or community without their permission.

I write this as an attempt to help people with limited understanding of a new-to-them experience, not to try to stereotype any individuals into boxes that none of us should ever be contained within.

Please forgive any offenses, and please feel free to reach out with any corrections.

Contents

Introduction: Welcome to the Rainbow Family

Hey there! Welcome to the beautiful world of Rainbow Connections! I'm Syd, and I'm super excited to have you here.

Grab a seat, get comfy, and let's chat. So, what's this book all about, you ask? Well, let me give you the lowdown.

This book is your go-to guide on how to be an awesome ally to your LGBTQIA+ friends and relatives. As a straight ally myself, I totally get where you're coming from.

You don't have to change who you are or how you treat your loved ones—it's all about understanding and supporting them where they are... and trust me, people tend to overcomplicate the experience of coming out!

Our LGBTQIA+ friends bring so much diversity, joy, and fabulousness to the world. They come in all shapes, sizes, and shades of the rainbow. From the fierce queens and kings to the non-binary and genderqueer folks, our rainbow family is colorful and unique, just like you and me.

Now, I know it can sometimes feel a little daunting to navigate this world if you haven't had much exposure to it. But fear not; we've got your back.

This book is here to equip you with the knowledge to help you embrace the news you may have recently received. You might also be curious so that you can be a great ally should someone come out to you in the future.

In these pages, we're gonna break down barriers with love, understanding, and maybe a little humor. We'll demystify the lingo of the LGBTQIA+ community, celebrate the beauty of diverse sexual orientations, and dive into the exciting world of gender identity.

We'll become communication ninjas, allies in action, and explore the ins and outs of relationships and intimacy. But above all, we'll celebrate the power of love and acceptance.

Now, here's the deal: being an ally doesn't mean you have to become an expert overnight or pretend to be someone you're not. We're all about keeping it real.

You're already an awesome person, and your willingness to learn and support your loved ones is what makes you an incredible ally.

So, get ready to rock your most comfortable jeans and grab a cup of your favorite brew because we're about to embark on an epic journey together.

Think of it as a fun adventure where we'll learn, grow, and create a world that's full of love, acceptance, and positive communication.

So, let's kick things off! The rainbow is waiting, and I know we're gonna have some fun along the way. Get ready for an awesome ride filled with learning, some laughter, compassion, and a whole lot of good vibes.

You're an amazing ally, and I'm thrilled to have you here. Let's do this!

Breaking the Ice: Coming Out and Communication

All right, buckle up! We're diving deep into the art of breaking the ice and nailing those conversations when someone comes out.

When prepared for this conversation, many people would likely handle it much better than they do when unprepared. Often, this conversation is a surprise, and when surprised, it's tougher to keep a focused mind.

My hope is that you are reading this book proactively and are already an ally by the time someone special to you opens up and 'comes out.' If not, and you got your hands on this book after the fact, that's okay too. It's never too late to say or do the right things.

Now, let's talk about the significance of the coming out process. Coming out takes courage. It's summoning the bravery to wear your most outrageous outfit to a party and saying, *"Hey, world, this is the real me!"*

It's a pivotal moment where your loved one is sharing a part of themselves that's been simmering beneath the surface.

When it comes to communication during this time, we've got some responses and scenarios to guide you.

Picture this: your friend or family member gathers everyone around, palms sweaty, and says those magical words, "I have something important to share. I'm [insert identity here]." It's like they've just dropped a beat, and now it's your turn to find your rhythm.

First things first — Do no harm. If you have held strong feelings against what you've just been told your loved one is now a part of, quick thinking on your part is key!

You need to, almost instantly, digest what you've just been told, do your best to hide any unintentional reactions and remind yourself that this person means something to you, and your first reaction could hurt them deeply.

Active listening is your secret weapon. It's all about being present, giving them your undivided attention, and leaving your distractions at the door.

Trust me, no Instagram story or funny cat video is as important as this moment. It's like when you're watching your favorite show, and your friend keeps interrupting with hilarious commentary—you want to be that engaged and supportive audience member.

Now, let's dive into the do's and don'ts of communication during this time. I've got your back, so here are a few pointers.

DO: Listen with Love and Laughter.

1. Put on your "Super Listener" cape and be prepared to lend an ear because your loved one is about to open up and share something truly special with you.

2. Activate your "Pause Button" and leave judgment at the door. Remember, this is their moment to express their truth, and your role is to provide a safe and supportive space for them.

3. Embrace your inner detective and ask questions, not to interrogate, but to show genuine curiosity and understanding. It's all about exploring their journey and learning more about who they are.

4. Engage your "Empathy Engine" and put yourself in their shoes. Seek to understand their emotions, challenges, and joys, and let empathy guide your responses.

5. Master the art of silence. Sometimes, the most powerful thing you can do is simply be present and give them space to share their thoughts and feelings.

6. Bring a box of tissues, not because you expect tears, but because emotional moments can happen. Tissues are like supportive hugs for their emotions.

7. Summon your "Unconditional Love Shield" and let it be your armor throughout the conversation. Remember, their identity doesn't change your love for them. You're in this together.

8. Keep the "Advice Monster" at bay. Instead of jumping in with solutions or opinions, focus on active listening and validating their experiences.

9. Offer reassurance and support, like a warm blanket on a chilly day. Let them

know that they're not alone and that you're there for them, no matter what.

10. Channel your inner comedian and sprinkle some light-heartedness into the conversation. Laughter can help ease tension and create a more relaxed atmosphere.

11. Celebrate their bravery and self-discovery. They are opening up to you because they trust you, and that's a testament to the strength of your relationship.

12. Prepare some celebratory confetti (real or imaginary) to symbolize the joy and excitement of this milestone. It's like a party for their authentic self.

13. Be a mirror, reflecting back their emotions and experiences. Show that you genuinely see and hear them, validating their feelings and thoughts.

14. Share your own vulnerabilities, creating a safe space for openness and connection. Remember, this is a conversation, not a monologue.

15. Shower them with acceptance and love, like a gentle rain that washes away doubts and fears. Let them know that they are cherished just as they are.

16. Ditch the distractions and give them your full attention. Put away the phone, turn off the TV, and create an uninterrupted space for heartfelt conversation.

17. Practice active listening, nodding your head, and maintaining eye contact. Show that you are fully present and engaged in their story.

18. Be prepared to learn and grow together. This conversation is an

opportunity for both of you to deepen your understanding and strengthen your bond.

19. Have a stash of celebratory treats on hand, like rainbow-colored candies or cookies, to mark this special occasion. It's a sweet way to commemorate their bravery.

20. Respect their timeline. Coming out is a deeply personal process, and everyone moves at their own pace. Allow them to share as much or as little as they feel comfortable with.

21. Create a secret handshake to symbolize your unwavering support. It can be a playful pact that says, "I've got your back, always."

22. Keep your heart open because their coming out is an invitation to embrace

diversity and broaden your own perspective. Love knows no bounds.

23. Use "I" statements to express your feelings and emotions. This conversation is about them, but sharing your own experiences can foster a deeper connection.

24. Show gratitude for their trust in confiding in you. Let them know how honored you feel to be part of their journey.

25. End the conversation with a group hug or a high-five, symbolizing the strength and love that binds you together. It's a shared moment of connection and affirmation.

Remember, this is just the beginning of an ongoing conversation. Embrace the journey, continue to communicate openly, and celebrate the beautiful person your loved one is becoming.

When your loved one opens up to you, the key is to listen with an open heart and a sense of humor.

Think of it like going to a comedy show—except this time, the comedian is sharing their life story, and they're counting on you to be their biggest fan.

So be there for them, laugh with them, and let them know they're supported every step of the way.

DON'T: Turn It into a One-Person Stand-Up Show.

1. Don't interrupt or talk over them – their story is like a thrilling novel, and you don't want to spoil the plot!

2. Avoid making it about yourself. This is their moment to shine. For this time, accept that you're the supporting character in their story.

3. Don't respond with clichés or empty platitudes. Keep those "inspirational quotes" locked away, as they might fall flat in this moment.

4. Refrain from jumping to conclusions or assuming you know their entire journey. Their truth may have many surprising twists and turns.

5. Don't try to fix them or suggest that they need fixing. They're not broken; they're embracing their authentic self.

6. Avoid asking invasive or inappropriate questions. Give them the space to share what they feel comfortable sharing.

7. Don't respond with judgment or disapproval. They're not seeking your critique; they're seeking your love and acceptance.

8. Avoid gossiping or sharing their story without their consent. Respect their privacy and honor the trust they've placed in you.

9. Don't minimize their experience or dismiss their feelings. Remember, this is a significant moment for them, and their emotions are valid.

10. Refrain from attempting to change their mind or convince them otherwise. This is their truth, and it deserves respect.

11. Avoid using humor as a defense mechanism or downplaying the seriousness of the conversation. This is a time for sincerity and empathy.

12. Don't make assumptions about their future choices or relationships. Let them explore and define their own path.

13. Refrain from projecting your fears or biases onto their experience. Listen with an open mind and heart.

14. Avoid sharing unsolicited opinions or advice. They have trusted you with their story, not their decision-making process.

15. Don't rush them or pressure them for immediate answers. Give them the time

and space they need to process their emotions.

16. Refrain from interrogating them about their past or demanding explanations. Trust that they will share what they're comfortable sharing.

17. Avoid using outdated or derogatory language. Be mindful of the words you choose and the impact they can have.

18. Don't assume that their identity defines their entire being. Remember, they are complex individuals with many facets to celebrate.

19. Refrain from imposing your expectations or societal norms onto their journey. This is their story, and they get to write it on their own terms.

20. Avoid making assumptions about their experiences based on stereotypes or

generalizations. Listen with an open mind and let them guide the narrative.

21. Don't use their coming out as gossip fodder or a topic for small talk. Treat their story with the respect it deserves.

22. Refrain from pressuring them to come out to others before they are ready. It's their journey, and they should decide who to share it with and when.

23. Avoid using dismissive language or invalidating their feelings. Show compassion and empathy throughout the conversation.

24. Don't make promises you can't keep. Be honest about your own journey of understanding and growth.

25. Lastly, don't forget to follow up with ongoing support and love. This conversation is just the beginning of a

deeper connection and continued acceptance.

Remember, every person and every conversation is unique. Approach each situation with empathy, respect, and a willingness to learn and grow.

Now, here's a tip: avoid turning this moment into a stand-up comedy routine. This isn't the time to unleash your repertoire of outdated punchlines or impersonations.

It's all about creating a safe and supportive space. Offer a genuine response, like a warm hug, a kind smile, or a heartfelt "Thank you for sharing this with me. I'm honored that you trust me."

But it doesn't stop there. It's crucial to practice empathy and create an open dialogue.

Here's how:

1. Develop your "Empathy Radar" and tune in to their emotions like a radio station. Show genuine interest in understanding their perspective. Put yourself in their fabulous shoes. Remember that coming out is a personal journey, and everyone experiences it differently. So, lead with empathy, understanding, and a big dose of kindness. Like when you're craving your favorite dessert, and your friend surprises you with an extra-large slice—it's all about that sweet gesture.

2. Master the art of active listening, which includes nodding, maintaining eye contact, and occasionally interjecting with supportive affirmations like "You've got this!"

3. Create a Safe Space: This is the secret sauce. You want to create a space where

they feel safe, loved, and accepted. Let them know that you're there to support them and that their journey matters to you. It's turning your home into a cozy sanctuary, complete with soft blankets and warm, welcoming vibes.

4. Embrace the power of "Mirror, Mirror" by reflecting their emotions back to them. This helps them feel heard and validated.

5. Cultivate a sense of shared vulnerability by opening up about your own experiences. This fosters trust and creates a safe space for open dialogue.

6. Practice the "Pause and Reflect" technique. Take a moment before responding to ensure your words are thoughtful and considerate.

7. Use humor as a bridge to ease tension and create a more relaxed atmosphere. Laughter can be a powerful tool to

connect on a deeper level. Just don't overdo it.

8. Be a "Feelings Translator" by empathetically expressing their emotions in words. It shows that you understand and care about their experience.

9. Prioritize non-verbal cues like gentle touches, reassuring hugs, or a comforting presence. Sometimes, actions can speak louder than words.

10. Create a "Safe Word" to use when conversations become overwhelming or intense. It allows both of you to take a step back and regroup before continuing.

11. Find common ground by discovering shared interests or hobbies. It can help foster a sense of connection and open avenues for further conversation.

12. Practice the art of compromise and finding a middle ground. Seek solutions that work for both of you, fostering a balanced and harmonious dialogue.

13. Be open to learning and evolving together. Approach conversations with a growth mindset, recognizing that both of you have unique perspectives to offer.

14. Use "I" statements to express your thoughts and feelings, keeping the focus on your own experiences rather than making assumptions about theirs.

15. Cultivate curiosity and genuine interest in their experiences. Approach conversations as an opportunity to learn and understand them on a deeper level.

16. Be patient and understanding, acknowledging that everyone processes information and emotions at their own

pace. Give them the time they need to express themselves fully.

17. Practice "Active Validation" by acknowledging their feelings and experiences without judgment. Let them know that their emotions are valid and worthy of respect.

18. Use visual aids like diagrams, drawings, or even emojis to communicate emotions and thoughts. Sometimes, a picture can speak volumes.

19. Step into their shoes by imagining yourself in their situation. This helps cultivate empathy and allows you to view things from their perspective.

20. Practice gratitude by expressing appreciation for their vulnerability and trust. Let them know how grateful you are for their willingness to open up and share.

21. Avoid interrupting or monopolizing the conversation. Give them ample space and time to express themselves fully.

22. Show interest in their well-being by asking about their self-care practices. It demonstrates your genuine concern for their emotional and mental health.

23. Celebrate milestones and progress along their journey. Acknowledge their growth and accomplishments, no matter how small they may seem.

24. Keep an open mind and be willing to challenge your own preconceived notions. Approach conversations with a sense of curiosity and a desire to learn.

25. End each conversation on a positive note, expressing your love and support. Let them know that you're there for them, no matter what.

Remember, this chapter is all about breaking the ice and building those essential communication skills.

By listening with love, avoiding stand-up comedy routines, and creating a safe space, you're well on your way to becoming a rockstar ally.

In the next chapter, we'll jump into the Terminology Tango, where we'll decode the vibrant language of the LGBTQIA+ community with a fun twist.

So, keep that positive energy flowing, and let's continue this fabulous rainbow ride together!

Terminology Tango: Decoding LGBT Vocabulary

In this chapter, we're diving headfirst into the world of LGBTQIA+ vocabulary. Get ready for a terminology tango that will have you strutting your stuff with confidence and understanding. Together, we'll decode the language of the rainbow community and celebrate the rich tapestry of identities within it.

Now, you might be thinking, "Syd, what's with all the acronyms? LGBTQ+, what does it all mean?" Well, let's break it down together.

The LGBTQIA+ acronym represents a diverse range of identities and experiences. Like a rainbow flag flying high, showcasing the beautiful spectrum of humanity. Let's take a closer look:

L: Lesbian - Women who are attracted to other women. It's having a favorite ice cream flavor and sticking to it. They know what they like, and they embrace it!

G: Gay - Men who are attracted to other men. Picture it as finding your groove on the dance floor. When the music starts playing, they feel that magnetic pull toward their fellow gentlemen.

B: Bisexual - Individuals who are attracted to both men and women. Like being at a buffet and appreciating all the delicious options on offer. Bisexual folks are all about embracing the diverse flavors of love.

T: Transgender - These amazing individuals have a gender identity that differs from the sex they were assigned at birth. It's finding the courage to be your truest, most authentic self. They're superheroes, living their truth and showing the world their inner strength.

Q: Queer - A term that's been reclaimed by the community. It's an umbrella term that encompasses various non-heterosexual and non-cisgender identities. Think of it as a bold statement, challenging norms and embracing uniqueness.

Note: Some may not prefer the term Queer, often older generations who felt the sting of the word when it was used as an insult. Be aware that allies should be sensitive to terms that may be unwelcome coming from someone outside the community.

Q: Questioning - Questioning refers to individuals who are in the process of exploring and questioning their own sexual orientation, gender identity, or both. It is a self-reflective phase where individuals are uncertain or exploring different aspects of their identity, seeking a deeper understanding of who they are and how they relate to their own sense of self and the world around them.

I: Intersex - A term used to describe individuals who are born with physical sex characteristics that do not fit typical definitions of male or female.

Intersex variations can involve chromosomal, gonadal, hormonal, or anatomical differences, which may not be immediately apparent at birth.

Intersex individuals have diverse experiences and identities, and they may choose to identify within the LGBTQIA+ community based on their own gender identity, sexual orientation, or personal connection to the broader queer community.

A: Asexual - Refers to individuals who experience little or no sexual attraction to others. They may still experience romantic, emotional, or affectionate attractions, but the absence of sexual attraction is a defining aspect of their orientation.

A: Aromantic - Refers to individuals who do not experience romantic attraction to others. Aromantic individuals may still experience sexual attraction or engage in sexual relationships, but they do not have a desire for romantic involvement or intimate partnerships in the traditional sense.

A: Agender - Refers to individuals who do not identify with or experience a gender identity. They may not feel a connection to the binary gender categories of male or female, or they may identify as having no gender at all.

Agender individuals may express their gender identity in various ways or choose not to conform to traditional gender expectations.

But wait, there's more! The "+" symbol represents the inclusivity of identities beyond the main acronym. It's a way of saying, "Hey, we see you, and you matter too!"

Now that we've got the lingo down, it's time to embrace the diversity within the LGBTQIA+ community. Just like a dazzling mosaic, we come together with different experiences, stories, and backgrounds. It's a beautiful symphony of humanity.

It's important to use inclusive and respectful language when talking about the LGBTQIA+ community. Don't worry, though. We're here to guide you on your linguistic journey. Here are a few tips to keep in mind:

Respect Preferred Terms: Everyone's journey is unique, and so are their preferred terms. If someone tells you how they identify, use those terms. It's receiving a VIP pass to their inner world—honored, trusted, and respected.

Ask with Care: Curiosity is natural but remember to ask questions with respect and genuine interest. If you're unsure about something, approach the conversation with an open heart and a willingness to learn. It's discovering a hidden gem in a conversation, expanding your knowledge and connection.

Evolve and Educate: Language is ever evolving, and it's okay to make mistakes. The important thing is to learn, grow, and adjust accordingly. Be open to new ideas, educate yourself about different identities and experiences, and support others on their journey. It's like adding new dance moves to your repertoire, staying in step with the changing rhythms of the world.

So, we've taken our first steps into the world of LGBTQIA+ terminology. We've embraced the diverse identities within our rainbow family and learned how to use language with respect and inclusivity.

In the next chapter, we'll dive into the rainbow spectrum of sexual orientations, where we'll explore the beauty of love and attraction. Get ready for a colorful adventure!

The Rainbow Spectrum: Sexual Orientation 101

We're about to explore the vibrant rainbow spectrum of sexual orientation. Get ready to bust some myths, embrace diversity, and celebrate the universal power of love and attraction. It's time to break out the confetti and let the colors shine!

Now, let's kick things off by debunking some common misconceptions. Picture this: you're at a party, and someone says, "All you need to know about sexual orientation is 'gay' or 'straight,' right?" O-M-G, we're about to rock their world!

Sexual orientation is much more complex. It's not just about "gay" or "straight"—it's a dazzling array of identities and attractions. Let's dive into some of the options:

L stands for Lesbian. Lesbian refers to women who are sexually attracted to other women. It celebrates the diverse expressions of love and intimacy between women, fostering a sense of empowerment and community within the LGBTQIA+ spectrum.

G stands for Gay. Gay is a term commonly used to describe individuals, both men, and women, who are sexually attracted to people of the same gender. It encompasses the rich tapestry of same-sex attraction and relationships, promoting self-acceptance, pride, and love.

B stands for Bisexual. Bisexual individuals are sexually attracted to both their own gender and other genders. Bisexuality recognizes the potential for attraction to multiple genders, highlighting the fluidity and range of human sexuality.

T stands for Transgender. Transgender individuals have a gender identity that does not align with the sex assigned to them at birth. In terms of sexuality, transgender individuals may identify as lesbian, gay, bisexual, or any other sexual orientation that aligns with their gender identity.

Q stands for Queer or Questioning. Queer is an umbrella term that encompasses diverse sexual orientations and gender identities outside of heterosexual norms. It celebrates the exploration and embrace of non-conventional sexualities and identities.

Questioning refers to individuals who are in the process of exploring and questioning their own sexual orientation, acknowledging the fluidity and self-discovery within the LGBTQIA+ community.

I stands for Intersex. Intersex individuals have physical sex characteristics that do not fit typical definitions of male or female. In terms of sexuality, intersex individuals can identify with any sexual orientation that aligns with their personal attractions and desires.

A stands for Asexual. Asexual individuals do not experience sexual attraction to others. They may have emotional, romantic, or platonic connections, but their sexuality does not include sexual attraction.

These definitions highlight the range of sexual orientations within the LGBTQIA+ community, promoting understanding, acceptance, and celebration of diverse expressions of sexuality and identity.

+ many more: The rainbow spectrum continues! There are identities like demisexual, which is experiencing sexual attraction after developing a strong emotional bond, and others that defy categorization. Each person's journey is unique and deserves respect and celebration.

Now, here's the magical truth: love and attraction are universal. It doesn't matter who you are or who you love; what matters is the genuine connection and joy that comes with it. Love doesn't have boundaries—it's an unstoppable force that brings people together.

Embracing diversity within the LGBTQIA+ community means recognizing that love knows no limits. It's like attending a vibrant carnival filled with different attractions, colors, and sounds. Each experience is unique, but the essence of joy and connection remains the same.

So, let's celebrate the beautiful tapestry of sexual orientations within the rainbow family. Break those stereotypes, embrace the vastness of possibilities, and remember that love is a language we all speak.

Gender Blender: Understanding Gender Identity

Now, we're diving headfirst into the world of gender identity. Get ready to embrace the complexities, celebrate personal expression, and dance to the beat of authenticity. It's time to unlock the magic of the gender blender!

Gender identity extends far beyond the binary, like a kaleidoscope of possibilities, where individuals explore and express their true selves. So, let's unravel this fascinating world together.

The Gender Spectrum: Picture a spectrum stretching from one end to the other, representing the diversity of gender identities. It's a vibrant rainbow, where each color represents a unique gender experience. Some people identify with the gender they were assigned at birth, while others don't.

The understanding of gender has evolved to encompass a wide spectrum of identities beyond the traditional binary concept of male and female.

While it is difficult to provide an exact number, as gender is a deeply personal and individual experience, there are numerous gender identities that people may identify with.

Some of these identities include:

Male: Identifying as a man or male.

Female: Identifying as a woman or female.

Non-binary: Identifying outside of or beyond the binary concept of male and female.

Agender: Having no gender or a lack of gender identity.

Bigender: Identifying with two genders, often experiencing them simultaneously or alternating between them.

Genderfluid: Experiencing a fluid or shifting gender identity that may change over time.

Demigender: Identifying partially, but not fully, with a particular gender.

Two-Spirit: A cultural and spiritual identity within certain Indigenous communities that encompasses the presence of both masculine and feminine qualities.

Androgynous: Having a gender expression that combines elements of both masculinity and femininity.

Neutrois: Identifying as a neutral or null gender, experiencing a sense of genderlessness.

Gender non-conforming: Rejecting or defying traditional gender norms and expectations.

Pangender: Feeling a connection to all genders or multiple genders.

Gender questioning: In the process of exploring and questioning one's gender identity.

Transgender is an empowering and affirming term that encompasses individuals whose gender identity does not align with the sex assigned to them at birth. It acknowledges and celebrates the journey of self-discovery, self-acceptance, and living authentically.

Transgender individuals are courageous trailblazers, embracing their true selves and expressing their gender identity in ways that align with their innermost feelings.

Transgender individuals navigate a profoundly personal and transformative journey, marked by self-reflection, self-acceptance, and often the pursuit of medical interventions or social transitions. Their identities are valid and deserving of respect and understanding.

It is essential to honor and respect each transgender individual's self-identified gender and preferred pronouns. By doing so, we affirm their identity and show our commitment to creating a more inclusive and compassionate society.

Non-binary is an inclusive term that encompasses individuals who do not exclusively identify as male or female within the gender binary. Non-binary individuals may identify as having a gender that is outside of or in between male and female, or they may reject the concept of gender altogether.

Non-binary individuals challenge norms, opening up conversations about gender diversity, inclusivity, and self-expression. They inspire us to reimagine and reshape our understanding of gender, encouraging a more fluid and accepting society.

By embracing non-binary identities, we create a world that recognizes and values the full spectrum of human gender experiences. It fosters inclusivity, respect, and a celebration of diverse identities, empowering individuals to live authentically without being confined to societal expectations.

Genderqueer is a term that embraces and celebrates individuals whose gender identity falls outside of the traditional binary concept of male and female. It is a self-affirming identity that challenges societal norms and allows individuals to explore and express their authentic selves in unique and empowering ways.

Genderqueer individuals often identify as being neither exclusively male nor female, or they may identify as both genders, as a combination of genders, or as a different gender entirely.

Now, here's the magical truth: gender identity is deeply personal. It's about being true to oneself and finding the courage to express that truth. Each person's journey is unique and deserves respect, understanding, and celebration.

When it comes to supporting our friends and loved ones on their gender identity journey, here are a few essential things to keep in mind:

Respect Preferred Pronouns: Pronouns matter. Use the pronouns that individuals prefer, whether it's "he," "she," "they," or something entirely unique. It's like having a special name that resonates with your true identity—using it shows love and acceptance.

Educate Yourself: Embrace the role of a lifelong learner. Educate yourself about different gender identities, experiences, and challenges. Listen to stories, read books and articles, and engage in respectful conversations. It's stepping into a library filled with knowledge and understanding, ready to expand your horizons.

Create Inclusive Spaces: Embrace diversity in all its forms. Create spaces where people feel safe, supported, and seen.

It's hosting a party where everyone feels welcome, from the introverts who prefer cozy corners to the extroverts who want to dance in the spotlight.

Remember, the journey of gender identity is a dance of self-discovery and self-expression.

By embracing the fluidity and beauty of gender, we create a world that celebrates and uplifts everyone.

Family Matters: Supporting LGBT Loved Ones

Now, let's dive into the wonderful world of supporting our LGBTQIA+ loved ones within the family dynamic. Family matters and being a supportive ally can make all the difference.

So, let's gather 'round the table, share some laughs, and explore how we can create a safe and loving environment for our rainbow family members.

Parental Concerns and Reactions: As a parent, it's natural to have concerns when your child comes out as LGBTQ+.

You might worry about their well-being, their happiness, or how they'll navigate the challenges they may face. It's stepping onto a roller coaster ride with a mix of excitement and uncertainty. But fear not; we're here to navigate those loops and turns together.

Sibling Solidarity and Support: Siblings, oh, how they have a unique bond! When your brother, sister, or sibling figure comes out, it's an opportunity to strengthen that connection even further.

It's like finding a secret treasure map and embarking on an adventure side by side. Embrace the role of a supportive sibling, offering love, understanding, and a listening ear. Together, you can conquer any challenge that comes your way.

Extended Family Dynamics: Ah, the wide web of extended family—filled with diverse personalities, quirky traditions, and plenty of love. When a family member comes out, it can sometimes stir the pot.

Imagine adding a new spice to your family recipe; it might take some getting used to, but it can enhance the flavor in unexpected ways.

Embrace the opportunity to educate and foster understanding among extended family members, showing them the beauty of acceptance.

Here are a few tips to help you navigate and support your LGBTQIA+ loved ones within the family:

Listen with an Open Heart: Your loved ones' experiences and emotions are valid. Take the time to listen attentively without judgment or assumptions. Envision having a heart-to-heart conversation, where you create a safe space for them to express themselves openly.

Educate Yourself and Others: Be the family advocate! Educate yourself about LGBTQIA+ issues, experiences, and history.

Share that knowledge with your family members, helping them understand and appreciate the uniqueness of their loved ones. You can be the family's own walking encyclopedia, spreading understanding and acceptance.

Practice Unconditional Love: Love knows no boundaries. Unconditional love means embracing your LGBTQIA+ loved ones just as they are without trying to change or "fix" them.

It's wrapping them in a warm, cozy blanket of acceptance, making them feel safe and cherished.

Celebrate Milestones and Achievements: From birthdays to graduations, celebrate the milestones of your LGBTQIA+ loved ones with joy and enthusiasm.

It's throwing the biggest party in town, complete with colorful decorations and an abundance of love. Show them that their accomplishments are valued and celebrated, just like anyone else's.

Remember, supporting our LGBTQIA+ loved ones within the family is a journey of love, understanding, and growth.

By creating a safe and accepting space, you'll foster a sense of belonging and empower them to thrive.

Let's keep spreading love and acceptance, one step at a time!

How to Become Part of the Support System

Let's dive into the essential role of being a part of the support system for your friend or loved one who has come out to you. It's time to remember that this journey is not about you; it's about them and their need for your unwavering support and love. So, let's put on our supportive hats and learn how to be the best ally we can be.

It's Not About You: First things first, remember that this is not about you. It's about your friend or loved one who has trusted you with their truth. They need to know that their coming out won't change your relationship. Show them that they're still loved, valued, and cherished, just as they were before they shared this part of themselves with you.

Ask How You Can Help: This is a fantastic time to ask your friend or loved one what they need from you. Be a superhero sidekick, ready to assist in any way possible. They might appreciate having someone to talk to, or they might need help navigating resources or connecting with support networks. Simply being there to listen can make a world of difference.

Do Your Research: Education is key. Take the initiative to educate yourself about the LGBTQ+ community, their experiences, and the challenges they face. Reading this book is a fantastic start! Understanding the terminology, history, and struggles can help you be a more informed and empathetic ally.

Be Their Safe Space: Create an environment where your friend or loved one feels safe to be themselves. It's having a cozy nook where they can relax and be free from judgment or prejudice. Show them that they can confide in you without fear of rejection or betrayal. Be their rock and their shelter in times of uncertainty.

Don't Change Your Opinion: Your loved one's sexual orientation or gender identity doesn't change who they are at their core. Don't let it change your opinion of them either. Like realizing they have a secret passion for karaoke—it's just an added layer that makes them even more interesting and unique. Embrace their truth and let it deepen your bond.

Now, let's dive into 25 small actions you can take to build a strong support system and become a trusted ally for the LGBT community and your friend:

1. Use inclusive language and pronouns.
2. Educate others about LGBT issues and challenges.

3. Attend LGBT events and celebrations.

4. Show visible support with Pride symbols or accessories.

5. Challenge discriminatory remarks or jokes.

6. Share positive stories and news about the LGBT community.

7. Listen with an open mind and heart.

8. Respect privacy and confidentiality.

9. Offer a shoulder to lean on during difficult times.

10. Advocate for LGBT rights and equality.

11. Celebrate their milestones and achievements.

12. Learn about LGBT history and pioneers.

13. Promote inclusive policies and practices in your workplace or community.

14. Amplify LGBT voices and stories through social media.

15. Encourage them to join LGBT support groups or organizations.

16. Offer to accompany them to LGBT events or gatherings.

17. Respect their boundaries and autonomy.

18. Support LGBT-owned businesses and artists.

19. Share resources and information about LGBT support services.

20. Challenge your own biases and stereotypes.

21. Support LGBT-inclusive media, literature, and art.

22. Stand up against bullying and discrimination.

23. Volunteer or donate to LGBT charities.

24. Be patient and understanding as they navigate their journey.

25. Love them unconditionally.

Remember, being a part of the support system means standing with your friend or loved one through thick and thin. Your small actions can make a big difference in their lives, showing them that they're not alone on this journey.

Let's build a network of support and become allies who uplift, understand, and celebrate the LGBTQ+ community.

In the next chapter, we'll explore the transformation from being an ally to becoming an advocate as we learn how to make a positive impact in the wider community.

Let's keep shining the light of love and acceptance together!

From Ally to Advocate: Making a Positive Impact

Okay, now we'll dive into the journey from being an ally to becoming an advocate for the LGBTQIA+ community. It's time to take our support to the next level and make a positive impact in the wider world. Get ready to channel your inner superhero, and let's go!

Embrace Your Voice: As an ally, your voice holds power. It's like having a microphone in your hands, ready to amplify the message of love and acceptance. Speak up against discrimination, challenge stereotypes, and promote understanding wherever you go. Let your voice be a force for positive change.

Educate and Engage: Knowledge is power. Take the time to educate yourself and others about LGBTQIA+ issues, history, and rights. Attend workshops, read books, and engage in respectful conversations. It's donning a pair of superhero glasses that reveal the hidden truths and perspectives of the LGBTQIA+ community.

Stand Up Against Injustice: Injustice has no place in our world, and it's time to take a stand. Be a fearless advocate, challenging discrimination and inequality wherever you encounter it. Imagine wearing a superhero suit and using your powers for good, fighting against the forces that seek to hurt others.

Support LGBTQIA+ Organizations: There are incredible organizations out there working tirelessly for LGBTQIA+ rights, support, and empowerment. Show your support by volunteering, donating, or spreading the word about their important work. It's joining forces with other superheroes to create a stronger, more inclusive world. Sometimes the simplest things, like resharing an organization's post on social media, can do the most good.

Be an Ally in Everyday Actions: Making a positive impact doesn't always require grand gestures. It can be found in small, everyday actions. Be an ally by using inclusive language, challenging harmful jokes, and creating safe spaces for everyone, sprinkling kindness and acceptance into every interaction, creating ripples of change.

Remember, being an ally is a continuous journey of growth and advocacy. Your actions, no matter how small, can create a ripple effect of change and acceptance. Let's continue spreading love and making a positive impact together!

Love is Love: Relationships and Intimacy in the LGBTQIA+ Community

We're about to explore the beautiful world of relationships and intimacy within the LGBTQIA+ community. Love knows no boundaries, and it's time to celebrate the diverse expressions of affection and connection. Get ready for heartwarming stories, a touch of humor, and a deeper understanding of the power of love.

Love in all its Forms: Love comes in many shapes and sizes. Whether it's romantic, platonic, or familial, the LGBTQIA+ community knows how to embrace and celebrate love. They're a vibrant bouquet of flowers, each bloom representing a unique connection. From lifelong partnerships to chosen families, the love within this community knows no bounds.

Think about it: Imagine for a moment that your child or relative comes out to you. One of the common things I hear is, "It's disgusting to imagine them having sex with another [guy, girl]."

My question is usually, "So, do you find yourself imagining them having sex with someone from the other sex?" Because, honestly, to me... That's disgusting too. Why are we imagining what goes on behind closed doors with anyone we aren't in a sexual relationship with?

What happens, sexually or non-sexually, between consenting adults really shouldn't be something that anyone gets involved with. Books like this would be entirely irrelevant if we all spent less time in other peoples' business and more time improving our own relationships.

Of course, I suspect that's precisely why you're reading this book. You want to make sure you do the most good, or at least the least harm, for the health of a relationship with your friend or loved one. Right? With that in mind, let's get back to education, and I'll hop off my soapbox.

Same-Sex Relationships: These partnerships are built on mutual respect, understanding, and shared experiences. It's having a dance partner who moves in perfect sync with you, creating a beautiful harmony. Let's celebrate the joy, commitment, and enduring love found within these relationships.

Non-Heteronormative Relationships: Love doesn't always fit into traditional boxes, and that's where *non-heteronormative relationships* shine. From polyamory to open relationships, the LGBTQIA+ community explores alternative relationship structures that work for them. It's creating a unique recipe for love, adding a pinch of adventure and a sprinkle of communication.

Celebrating Individual Journeys: Every person's journey in relationships and intimacy is unique. Some may find love early in life, while others take their time, embarking on a road trip without a predetermined destination—enjoying the scenery, taking detours, and finding unexpected gems along the way.

Navigating Challenges: Just like any other relationship, LGBTQIA+ partnerships face challenges. It's essential to address and overcome obstacles together with open communication, empathy, and a splash of humor. It's like a dance routine—sometimes you stumble, but with a bit of laughter and supportive teamwork, you'll find your rhythm again.

Remember, love, is love, and it transcends all boundaries. By embracing and celebrating the diversity of relationships within the LGBTQIA+ community, we foster a world where everyone can love and be loved freely.

If you struggle with accepting this part of your loved one's life, ask yourself, would you prefer they live a life without love or hope for a loving relationship?

We all struggle to find the right partner. Why bind the hands and hearts of people who just want to love and be loved?

Love Knows No Bounds: Relationships and Intimacy

Let's delve into the world of relationships and intimacy without boundaries. Love knows no limits, and within the LGBTQIA+ community, it takes on many vibrant forms. Get ready to explore the dynamics of diverse relationships, challenge misconceptions, and celebrate the universal language of love, commitment, and intimacy.

Love in All Its Colors: Love is a kaleidoscope of emotions and connections. Within the LGBTQIA+ community, we celebrate a diverse range of relationships that reflect the full spectrum of human experience. Whether it's same-sex partnerships, polyamorous relationships, or any other beautiful arrangement, love finds its way to flourish.

Same-Sex Relationships: Let's shine a spotlight on same-sex relationships, shall we? These partnerships are built on love, respect, and shared experiences. It's dancing with your favorite partner, moving together in perfect harmony. Let's celebrate the joy, commitment, and unwavering love found within these relationships.

Dispelling Misconceptions: Ah, those persistent misconceptions. It's time to address them head-on. Contrary to what some may think, same-sex relationships are not defined by stereotypes or roles. They're like a unique dance routine choreographed by love, where both partners contribute their authentic selves. It's all about mutual respect, shared values, and emotional connection.

Beyond Monogamy: Love doesn't always fit into a one-size-fits-all mold. The LGBTQIA+ community explores various relationship styles beyond monogamy, such as polyamory or open relationships. It's having a canvas that allows for multiple brushstrokes, creating a masterpiece of love and understanding. These relationships are grounded in honest communication, trust, and mutual consent.

Universal Aspects of Love: While relationships within the LGBTQIA+ community may have their unique dynamics, there are universal aspects that transcend labels and orientation. Love is love, and it thrives on communication, trust, and support. It's a symphony where different instruments come together to create a beautiful melody. These universal qualities are the building blocks of strong and fulfilling relationships.

Now, let's address some common questions that often arise:

"But don't same-sex relationships lack gender roles?" Gender roles are not prerequisites for love. Same-sex relationships thrive on authentic connections, mutual support, and shared experiences. There's no need to conform to societal expectations because love and commitment are not bound by rigid roles.

"How can non-monogamous relationships work?" Non-monogamous relationships require open communication, trust, and mutual consent. It's like an ongoing conversation where all partners involved define their boundaries, expectations, and desires. It's important to remember that the key to any successful relationship lies in understanding and respecting each other's needs.

"What about long-term commitment?" Long-term commitment is just as present in

LGBTQIA+ relationships as in any other. Love knows no bounds, and within the LGBTQIA+ community, you'll find enduring partnerships that stand the test of time. It's planting a tree whose roots grow deeper and stronger over the years.

I feel compelled to throw in that open communication, trust, and mutual consent is vital to every relationship, not only those within the LGBTQIA+ community. It only takes recalling that the divorce rate is commonly quoted at almost 50% of each marriage ends in divorce.

Could it be argued that those who are the loudest against the LGBTQIA+ community may well reside within that demographic? Possibly. As a straight, divorced person, I recognize that I'm not the master of relationships, and certainly will be the last to throw stones at anyone who's trying to navigate this life in search of mutual love and respect with others.

One other thing worth mentioning is that the divorce rate seems to be trending downward as the LGBTQIA+ community seems to be trending upward in numbers. New marriages also seem to be decreasing.

Could it be that as more people realize they cannot live happily in unfulfilling relationships, they choose to step out of the shadows of fear or social expectation and focus on finding their own happiness? I'd argue yes.

In the end, what truly matters is the love, respect, and happiness shared between partners. LGBTQIA+ relationships are like any other, filled with joy, challenges, and growth. By embracing their diversity, we expand our understanding of love itself.

A Rainbow Future: Progress and Hope

We'll reflect on the progress made in LGBTQIA+ rights and look to the future with hope and determination. It's time to celebrate how far we've come and envision a brighter, more inclusive world. So, let's dive in and paint a picture of a rainbow-filled future.

Celebrating Progress: Take a moment to acknowledge the incredible progress that has been made in LGBTQIA+ rights. From marriage equality to anti-discrimination laws, we've come a long way. It's watching a phoenix rise from the ashes, symbolizing resilience and triumph over adversity. Let's celebrate the milestones and the courageous individuals who paved the way for a more inclusive world.

Embracing Intersectionality: In our rainbow family, we must recognize the importance of intersectionality. LGBTQIA+ individuals exist within various social, cultural, and ethnic contexts.

It's a mosaic of identities, each piece contributing to the vibrant whole. Let's uplift and support those who face multiple forms of discrimination, ensuring that our fight for equality encompasses everyone.

Promoting Acceptance and Inclusion: Our journey doesn't end with progress; it continues with a commitment to acceptance and inclusion, planting seeds of love and understanding, nurturing them as they grow into a garden of equality. Let's challenge prejudice, create safe spaces, and foster a society where everyone is celebrated for their authentic selves.

Supporting LGBTQIA+ Youth: The youth are the future, and it's crucial to support and empower LGBTQIA+ young people. They hold the power to shape a more inclusive world. It's handing them a paintbrush, encouraging them to add their unique colors and brushstrokes to the canvas of progress. Let's provide resources, mentorship, and safe environments for them to thrive.

Spreading Love and Hope: Love is our superpower. Let's use it to inspire change and create a world where love and acceptance prevail. Envision a ripple effect, starting small but growing into a wave of transformation. Let's share stories, uplift voices, and spread hope to every corner of the world.

Remember that the journey doesn't stop here. It's an ongoing process of learning, growth, and allyship.

Historical Timeline of the LGBT Journey:

Year **Event**

1869   The term "homosexual" is coined by Karl Heinrich Ulrichs.

1897   Magnus Hirschfeld opens the first Institute for Sexual Science in Berlin.

1924   The first gay rights organization in the United States, the Society for Human Rights, is founded by Henry Gerber.

1935   The Nazis pass the Reich's Criminal Code, which criminalizes homosexuality.

1969   The Stonewall riots, a series of violent demonstrations by LGBT people against a police raid in New York City, are considered to be the start of the modern LGBT rights movement.

1973   The American Psychiatric Association removes

homosexuality from its list of mental disorders.

1977   The first gay pride parade is held in New York City.

1981   The AIDS epidemic begins.

1987   The first national LGBT rights organization in the United States, the Human Rights Campaign, is founded.

1993   The Supreme Court of the United States rules in the case of Lawrence v. Texas that laws against sodomy are unconstitutional.

2003   The United States Congress passes the Matthew Shepard and James Byrd Jr. Hate Crimes Prevention Act, which expands the federal definition of hate crimes to include crimes motivated by a victim's sexual orientation or gender identity.

2009   President Barack Obama signs the Don't Ask, Don't Tell Repeal Act of

2010, which allows openly gay and lesbian people to serve in the United States military.

2015 The Supreme Court of the United States rules in the case of Obergefell v. Hodges that same-sex marriage is a constitutional right.

2016 The United States Congress passes the Equality Act, which would prohibit discrimination on the basis of sexual orientation and gender identity in employment, housing, public accommodations, education, credit, and federal funding.

2022 President Joe Biden signs same-sex marriage bill into law.

This is just a brief overview of the LGBT journey. There are many other important events that have taken place throughout history, and the fight for LGBT rights is still ongoing.

Sources

1. www.playwrightshorizons.org/shows/trailers/backstory-log-cabin/
2. vermilioncountyfirst.com/2021/02/25/rep-miller-criticizes-house-democrats-legislation/
3. www.demos.org/blog/fight-homophobia-we-need-workplace-rights

Noteworthy Pioneers in the LGBT Movement

Magnus Hirschfeld (1868-1935): Hirschfeld was a German physician and sexologist who founded the Scientific-Humanitarian Committee in 1897, one of the first LGBT rights organizations. He advocated for the decriminalization of homosexuality and worked to challenge societal attitudes through research and education.

Harry Hay (1912-2002): Hay was an American gay rights activist who co-founded the Mattachine Society in 1950, one of the earliest homophile organizations in the United States. He played a significant role in organizing the LGBT community and laying the foundation for future activism.

Del Martin (1921-2008) and Phyllis Lyon (1924-2020): This power couple co-founded the Daughters of Bilitis in 1955, the first lesbian civil and political rights organization in the United States. They were instrumental in fighting for lesbian visibility and advocating for legal protections.

Marsha P. Johnson (1945-1992): Johnson was a transgender woman of color and a prominent figure in the Stonewall uprising of 1969, which marked a turning point in the LGBT rights movement. She co-founded the Street Transvestite Action Revolutionaries (STAR) and tirelessly advocated for transgender rights.

Harvey Milk (1930-1978): Milk was an American politician and the first openly gay elected official in California. He served as a member of the San Francisco Board of Supervisors and fought for LGBTQ+ rights, becoming an iconic figure in the movement until his tragic assassination in 1978.

Sylvia Rivera (1951-2002): Rivera was a transgender activist and a key figure in the Stonewall uprising. She co-founded STAR with Marsha P. Johnson and dedicated her life to fighting for the rights of transgender and homeless individuals.

Barbara Gittings (1932-2007): Gittings was a prominent American LGBT rights activist and organizer. She played a vital role in the early gay rights movement, advocating for the inclusion of homosexuality in the American Psychiatric Association's Diagnostic and Statistical Manual of Mental Disorders.

Larry Kramer (1935-2020): Kramer was an American playwright, author, and LGBT rights activist. He co-founded the Gay Men's Health Crisis (GMHC) in 1982, one of the first organizations dedicated to HIV/AIDS advocacy and support. His activism helped raise awareness and push for better medical treatments.

Edie Windsor (1929-2017): Windsor was a prominent LGBT rights activist and plaintiff in the landmark Supreme Court case United States v. Windsor in 2013. Her case led to the overturning of the Defense of Marriage Act (DOMA) and played a pivotal role in the push for marriage equality in the United States.

Audre Lorde (1934-1992): Lorde was an influential African American lesbian poet, writer, and civil rights activist. Her works, such as "Sister Outsider" and "Zami: A New Spelling of My Name," explored the intersections of race, gender, and sexuality. Lorde advocated for intersectionality within the feminist movement, emphasizing the importance of recognizing and addressing multiple forms of oppression.

Bayard Rustin (1912-1987): Rustin was a key organizer of the Civil Rights Movement in the United States and a gay rights advocate. He played a significant role in planning the 1963 March on Washington, where Martin Luther King Jr. delivered his famous "I Have a Dream" speech. Rustin's activism and commitment to nonviolence shaped the fight for equality on multiple fronts.

Ellen DeGeneres (born 1958): DeGeneres is an American comedian, actress, and television host who came out as a lesbian in 1997. Her decision to openly embrace her sexual orientation on her sitcom "Ellen" and in her personal life made her a trailblazer for LGBTQ+ visibility in mainstream media. DeGeneres has used her platform to advocate for equality and support various LGBT causes.

Frank Kameny (1925-2011): Kameny was an American gay rights activist and one of the first to fight against the U.S. government's discriminatory policies towards homosexuals. He led protests, filed lawsuits, and co-founded the Mattachine Society of Washington, D.C., advocating for equal treatment and an end to employment discrimination based on sexual orientation.

RuPaul Charles (born 1960): RuPaul is an American drag queen, actor, and TV personality known for hosting the reality show "RuPaul's Drag Race." Through his platform, RuPaul has brought drag culture into the mainstream and advocated for self-expression and acceptance. He has been an influential figure in spreading awareness and understanding of the LGBTQ+ community.

Jeanne Cordova (1948-2016): Cordova was a Chicana lesbian feminist, journalist, and community organizer. She co-founded the Lesbian Tide, a groundbreaking lesbian feminist magazine, and was an active participant in various LGBT and feminist organizations. Cordova worked tirelessly to amplify marginalized voices within the lesbian community and fought for social justice.

George Takei (born 1937): Takei is an American actor, best known for his role as Hikaru Sulu in the original "Star Trek" series. Takei came out publicly as gay in 2005 and has since become an outspoken advocate for LGBTQ+ rights, using his platform to raise awareness and promote inclusivity.

Kate Bornstein (born 1948): Bornstein is a gender non-conforming author, playwright, and performance artist. Their works, such as "Gender Outlaw: On Men, Women, and the Rest of Us," have challenged traditional notions of gender and inspired conversations about gender identity and expression.

Laverne Cox (born 1972): Cox is an American actress, producer, and transgender rights advocate. She gained recognition for her role as Sophia Burset in the series "Orange Is the New Black" and has used her platform to raise awareness about transgender issues, including the discrimination and violence faced by transgender individuals.

James Baldwin (1924-1987): Baldwin was an American novelist, playwright, and activist whose works explored themes of race, sexuality, and identity. He used his writing to shed light on the experiences of marginalized communities, including the LGBTQ+ community, and advocated for equality and social justice.

Christine Jorgensen (1926-1989): Jorgensen was an American transgender woman who gained international attention in the 1950s as one of the first individuals to undergo gender confirmation surgery. Her openness about her transition helped raise awareness and challenge societal misconceptions about gender identity.

Cleve Jones (born 1954): Jones, previously mentioned for his work in the AIDS epidemic, also played a significant role in LGBTQ+ activism as the creator of the AIDS Memorial Quilt. The quilt, consisting of individual panels honoring those lost to the disease, became a powerful symbol of remembrance, activism, and solidarity.

Chavela Vargas (1919-2012): Vargas was a Mexican singer and icon who defied traditional gender roles and openly expressed her lesbian identity. Through her music, she captivated audiences and broke barriers, becoming an inspiration for queer artists and individuals around the world.

These individuals, through their activism, art, advocacy, and bravery, have made significant contributions to the LGBT movement, advancing the rights and visibility of the community while inspiring generations to come.

Their courage and activism have paved the way for progress, inspiring future generations to continue the fight for justice and inclusivity.

Why the World Needs Individuality- A Parable

Once upon a time, in a land known as Harmonyville, there existed a peculiar community where everyone looked and acted exactly the same. From their neat haircuts to their symmetrical smiles, the people of Harmonyville seemed to have been molded from a cookie-cutter.

They had matching clothes, shared the same hobbies, and even spoke with identical voices. It was as if the town had been trapped in a never-ending sea of sameness.

Now, despite the picturesque appearance of Harmonyville, there was an undercurrent of monotony that flowed through the lives of its residents. Every day was a repetitive cycle of predictable routines. The townsfolk couldn't tell each other apart, and their conversations lacked depth and intrigue. It was as if their individuality had been locked away in a forgotten chest, buried deep within their hearts.

One day, a mischievous outsider named Jasper stumbled upon the town of Harmonyville. Jasper was a curious creature adorned with multicolored feathers and a mischievous twinkle in his eye.

He had traveled far and wide, encountering various cultures and diverse beings. Jasper was a reminder that the world was not meant to be a monotonous parade of conformity.

As Jasper explored Harmonyville, he couldn't help but notice the lack of diversity. The people looked like mirror images of one another, blending into the background like a sea of gray. Determined to bring some vibrancy into their lives, Jasper began to sing a joyful tune filled with playful sarcasm and mischief.

His song spread through the air, catching the attention of the townsfolk. They looked around in bewilderment, their identical faces mirroring a sense of curiosity.

The music was infectious, and slowly but surely, the people of Harmonyville began to sway and dance. As they moved, their rigid expressions softened, and a spark of individuality began to flicker within each of them.

Jasper's song carried a message of celebration for their differences. He sang of the beauty that lies in uniqueness, of the freedom to embrace one's quirks and idiosyncrasies.

With every note, the people of Harmonyville began to shed their uniformity, revealing a kaleidoscope of colors, talents, and personalities.

The town transformed into a vibrant tapestry of diversity. The once-identical individuals found joy in discovering their passions, expressing their opinions, and appreciating the differences that made them truly unique. No longer bound by conformity, the people of Harmonyville reveled in their newfound individuality.

Gone were the days of monotony and predictability. The streets of Harmonyville were filled with laughter, creativity, and a renewed zest for life. Each person contributed their own piece to the collective puzzle, creating a mosaic of perspectives, ideas, and talents.

Harmonyville had become a place where every person was valued for who they truly were rather than being defined by their appearance or conforming to societal expectations.

And so, the parable of Harmonyville teaches us that diversity is the essence of life. It is through our differences that we discover our true selves and connect with one another on a deeper level.

Embracing our individuality and celebrating the uniqueness of others brings forth a symphony of colors, melodies, and ideas that enriches the world around us.

So, let us dance to the rhythm of our own hearts, for it is in our diversity that we find harmony.

Pride and Prejudice: Dealing with Homophobia

Let's talk about the challenging topic of homophobia. It's time to confront prejudice head-on, handle negative reactions with grace, and foster a world of acceptance and understanding. So, let's stand tall and face homophobia with pride.

Confronting Homophobia with Humor: Laughter can be a powerful weapon against ignorance and prejudice. It's a shield that deflects negativity and brings light to dark situations. When faced with homophobia, a well-timed joke or witty response can challenge stereotypes and make people reflect on their biases without forcing confrontation or judgment. Remember, humor can be a powerful tool for education and breaking down barriers.

Handling Negative Reactions: We can't control the reactions of others. Some people may respond negatively to the LGBTQIA+ community, fueled by fear, ignorance, or personal beliefs. When faced with such negativity, it's important to remain calm and collected. Choose your battles wisely. Sometimes, it's more productive to engage in constructive dialogue, while other times, it's best to prioritize your own well-being and walk away from toxic environments.

Educating Others: Education is a powerful tool in combating homophobia. Share your experiences, personal stories, and knowledge to dispel myths and misconceptions. Empathy is key. By fostering understanding and compassion, we can help others see the human side of the LGBTQIA+ community and challenge their preconceived notions. Remember, change often happens one conversation at a time.

Building Resilience: Homophobia can be hurtful, but it doesn't define who a person is or diminish their worth. Building resilience is like flexing a muscle—it takes time and practice. Surround yourself with supportive allies, engage in self-care, and focus on your own personal growth. Remember, you are deserving of love, respect, and acceptance, regardless of others' opinions.

Fostering Acceptance: As allies, it's our responsibility to foster acceptance and create safe spaces for the LGBTQIA+ community. We can challenge homophobia through education, sharing personal stories, and promoting empathy. By amplifying the voices of marginalized individuals, we can cultivate understanding and encourage others to question their prejudices.

Allies in Action: Stand up and be an ally in action. Support LGBTQIA+ organizations, attend Pride events, and use your platform to raise awareness. Engage in conversations with friends, family, and colleagues to debunk myths and promote inclusivity. Small acts of allyship can make a big impact in creating a more accepting and supportive society.

Remember, homophobia is a reflection of ignorance and fear, not a reflection of a person's worth or the worth of the LGBTQIA+ community. Stay proud, stand tall, and surround yourself with a network of support. Together, we can challenge homophobia, celebrate diversity, and create a world where everyone is embraced for their true selves.

A Lifetime of Love: Celebrating LGBT Lives

As we begin to wrap up our journey toward understanding a world that you may have been unaware of until now, it's time to celebrate the fact that you care enough about at least one person who now resides within this community you've just researched.

Milestones and Festivities: Within the LGBT community, there are countless milestones and festivities worth celebrating. From Pride parades to National Coming Out Day, these occasions offer opportunities for joy, reflection, and empowerment. It can be like attending the most fabulous party of the year, where love, diversity, and acceptance are the guest of honor.

Embracing Diversity: Our celebrations are diverse identities, experiences, and expressions. It's a beautiful mosaic, where every piece contributes to the overall masterpiece. Embrace the richness of our community, appreciating the various shades of love, resilience, and triumph that make us who we are.

Creating Inclusive Environments: Let's spread the celebration beyond the boundaries of the LGBT community. As allies, it's our responsibility to create inclusive environments where everyone feels seen, valued, and loved. Imagine hosting a party where everyone is invited, and no one has to hide their true selves. By promoting acceptance and understanding, we create spaces where love can flourish.

The Power of Love and Acceptance: Love is the driving force behind our celebrations. It's a bright torch that guides us through the darkest of times. By embracing love and acceptance, we foster an environment where individuals can thrive, be proud of their authentic selves, and forge deep connections with others. It's in these connections that we find strength, support, and a sense of belonging.

Lifelong Connections: The bonds formed within the LGBT community are often unbreakable. It's discovering a chosen family, where friendships transform into lifelong connections. We celebrate the resilience, support, and unconditional love shared among individuals who have faced similar challenges. These connections remind us that we are not alone on our journeys and that together, we can overcome any obstacle.

As we close this chapter and our book comes to an end, let's reflect on the journey we've taken together. We've explored the complexities of sexual orientation and gender identity, learned how to be supportive allies, and confronted homophobia with humor and resilience. We've celebrated milestones, embraced the power of love, and fostered inclusive environments. But our journey doesn't end here. It continues in the choices we make, the conversations we have, and the love we share.

Let's carry the spirit of this book forward, championing acceptance and creating a world where everyone can love and be loved without fear or judgment. Together, we can make a lasting impact, one person, one community at a time.

Thank you for joining me on this incredible adventure. Remember, you have the power to be a beacon of love and acceptance in your own circles. Let's continue spreading joy, celebrating diversity, and embracing the beauty of LGBT lives. Love knows no bounds, so let's keep dancing to the rhythm of acceptance and live a lifetime of love.

You can now celebrate the historical milestones within the LGBT community and create inclusive environments, promote acceptance, and honor the incredible journeys of LGBT lives. You may choose to become an ally or even an advocate.

Even if you are only an ally with the one person who came out to you and prompted you to start doing some self-education, it's awesome that you care enough about them to reserve judgment and focus on understanding and holding onto that relationship.

Some people need some time to wrap their minds around what they've learned when someone comes out to them. You should absolutely spend some time letting it all sink in. That said, remember that your loved one is the same person they were before they trusted you with this information.

Everything is the same as before... they just chose to entrust you with a personal part of their lives because you mean enough to them that they want to be able to be open and honest with you.

So, let's raise our rainbow flags and dance with exuberance as we celebrate love and unity.

About the Author

Sydney founded the "I'm the Writer–Publishing Professional" certification program to properly train ghostwriters and freelancers to provide top-notch, income-generating services for their clients.

Through her experience as a publisher and someone who hires freelance writers, ghostwriters, and virtual assistants on a regular basis, she found that the market was flooded with applicants who had little or no skills to properly help a client.

Those who did have skills were diamonds in the rough, leaving her to recognize the intense need for a certification program that confirms that a graduate will have been verified to have completed all of the criteria needed to deliver quality stories and other deliverables such as graphics, videos, content creation, and general virtual assistance.

https://www.writercertification.com

Also From TLM Publishing House

FICTION –

Sydney Brown Presents Series
https://www.amazon.com/dp/B0BSBT36HN

The Mall Cadet Series
https://www.amazon.com/gp/product/B0B66
MDK3T

All In or Nothing Series
https://www.amazon.com/dp/B0B7FW9W8M

The 7 Wishes Series
https://www.amazon.com/dp/B0B62XJY59

The Deception Series
https://www.amazon.com/dp/B0B5RNQMF1

The Forbidden Love Series (18+)
https://www.amazon.com/dp/B0B5SX24SX

NONFICTION –

How to Start It Series
https://www.amazon.com/dp/B09Y2QHDPM